a smart girl's guide

Manners

the secret to grace, confidence,
and being your best

by Nancy Holyoke
illustrated by Julia Bereciartu

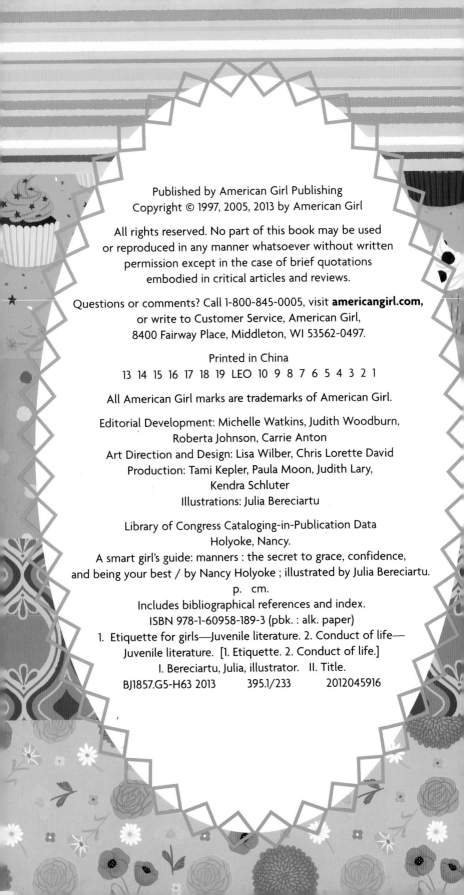

Published by American Girl Publishing
Copyright © 1997, 2005, 2013 by American Girl

Questions or comments? Call 1-800-845-0005, visit **americangirl.com,**
or write to Customer Service, American Girl,
8400 Fairway Place, Middleton, WI 53562-0497.

Printed in China
13 14 15 16 17 18 19 LEO 10 9 8 7 6 5 4 3 2 1

All American Girl marks are trademarks of American Girl.

Editorial Development: Michelle Watkins, Judith Woodburn,
Roberta Johnson, Carrie Anton
Art Direction and Design: Lisa Wilber, Chris Lorette David
Production: Tami Kepler, Paula Moon, Judith Lary,
Kendra Schluter
Illustrations: Julia Bereciartu

Library of Congress Cataloging-in-Publication Data
Holyoke, Nancy.
A smart girl's guide: manners : the secret to grace, confidence,
and being your best / by Nancy Holyoke ; illustrated by Julia Bereciartu.
p. cm.
Includes bibliographical references and index.
ISBN 978-1-60958-189-3 (pbk. : alk. paper)
1. Etiquette for girls—Juvenile literature. 2. Conduct of life—
Juvenile literature. [1. Etiquette. 2. Conduct of life.]
I. Bereciartu, Julia, illustrator. II. Title.
BJ1857.G5-H63 2013   395.1/233   2012045916

Dear Reader,

You're getting older. You're going new places and doing new things. You have more independence—and more responsibility, too. Suddenly everybody expects you to act more like an adult and less like your little sister. But that's not always easy to do.

Manners can help. Manners are commonsense guidelines for getting along with other people. They prevent you from being selfish and annoying. They remind you to be kind. They make you better company—and a better person. A girl with nice manners gets respect because she gives it. She's also got the tools to handle all kinds of situations. She finds confidence she never knew she had.

This book was first published some years ago as *Oops! The Manners Guide for Girls.* This edition has some new information, new pictures, and a new title. We hope you enjoy the book. We hope you use what you learn here, too. Every girl has what it takes to wow the world. Manners can help you do just that.

Your friends at American Girl

contents

PEOPLE
will look
AT YOUR MANNERS
AND
MAKE UP
their minds.

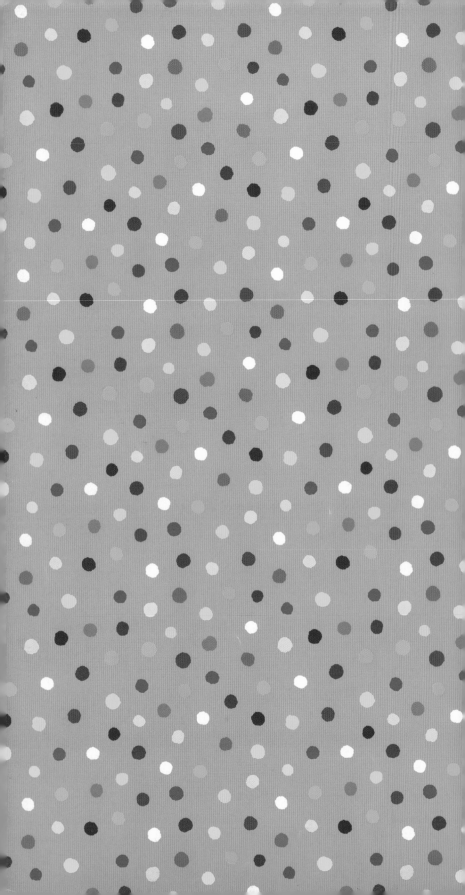

and finally . . .

the checklist

The ultimate test of good manners isn't which fork you use or how straight you sit. It's how you're able to answer questions like these. Check the box if the answer is yes.

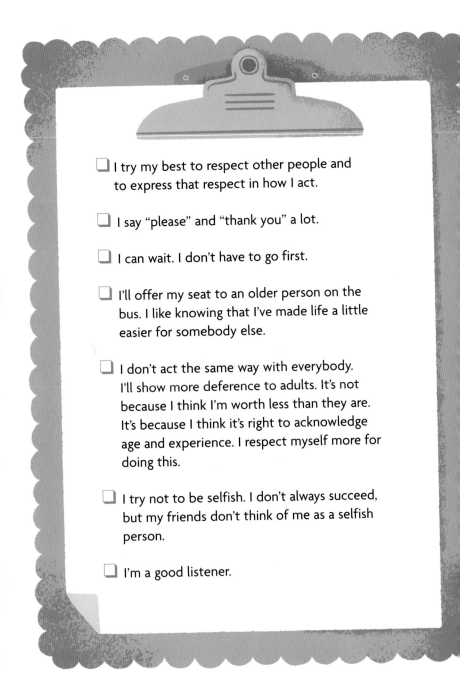

☐ I try my best to respect other people and to express that respect in how I act.

☐ I say "please" and "thank you" a lot.

☐ I can wait. I don't have to go first.

☐ I'll offer my seat to an older person on the bus. I like knowing that I've made life a little easier for somebody else.

☐ I don't act the same way with everybody. I'll show more deference to adults. It's not because I think I'm worth less than they are. It's because I think it's right to acknowledge age and experience. I respect myself more for doing this.

☐ I try not to be selfish. I don't always succeed, but my friends don't think of me as a selfish person.

☐ I'm a good listener.

☐ People trust me. They know I will keep my promises, protect their confidences, and respect their privacy.

☐ If I've made a mistake or I'm in the wrong, I apologize. I take responsibility for my actions.

☐ I do what I can to be a good host and a good guest.

☐ I may not love writing thank-you notes, but I write them.

☐ I know the difference between being well-mannered and being a doormat. I'm not afraid to speak up for what I believe in, and I can say no when I need to.

☐ I try not to wreck experiences for other people or cause them additional worry or work.

☐ People tend to feel better for having crossed paths with me—not worse.

Chances are, the more checks you made, the happier you are with yourself. And with all those checks you *should* be happy. Look at you! You're a person other people want to be around. You make the world better wherever you go.

And the bonus is this: You've got poise. You know the rules of the game. You feel easy and self-assured in new situations. You trust yourself. When the Queen gets wind of your marvelous manners and asks you to tea, you can walk into the palace ready to have a good time, knowing you can handle it. Your manners have given you confidence and grace. It didn't happen overnight. It happened because you use those very same manners with your family and friends every day.

Write to us!

At American Girl, we love hearing
from girls just like you. Tell us what you
think of *A Smart Girl's Guide: Manners.*
Send us your questions and ideas.

Write to us at

***Manners* Editor**

American Girl

8400 Fairway Place

Middleton, WI 53562

Here are some other American Girl books you might like:

the basics

me first?

There's a voice inside each of us that says

"Me first."

It tells us to please ourselves—to take what we want and do what we like, never mind about anybody else. If "me first" had its way, we'd spend our days trampling on one another's rights and feelings, and pretty soon the world would be a snarling mess.

This is where manners come in.

Manners aren't a bunch of rules dreamed up by fusspots who want to cramp your style. Manners help people get along together. They make us nicer. They teach us to put ourselves in the other person's shoes.

A girl who chooses to use good manners is telling the world she believes that other people matter as much as she does. She's saying that life isn't about what one person does for herself but about what people can do together for the common good.

So who decides what's polite and what's not? We all do.

When we talk about manners, we're talking about how most people in a certain time and place think people should behave. What's polite in one country isn't always polite in another. What was rude fifty years ago isn't always rude today. Manners depend a lot on custom—and different customs often live side by side.

In a way, manners are not so much a set of rules as they are a language you use to tell other people what they can expect from you. The better you know the language, the more you can say.

Are you trustworthy?

Do you think only of yourself?

Would you make a good friend or a poor one?

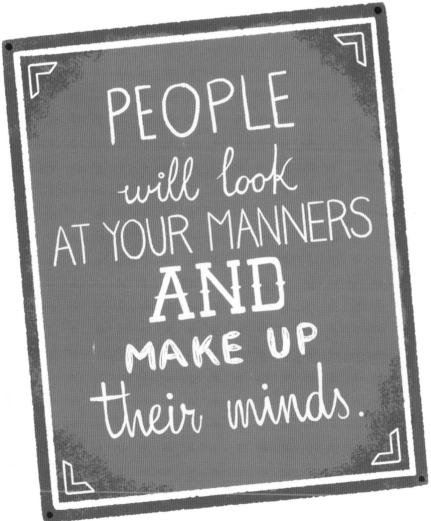

PEOPLE will look AT YOUR MANNERS AND MAKE UP their minds.

after you

The way you talk with a good friend when you're flopped on the grass is very different from the way you talk to the principal in the hallway at school. You change your style without thinking. And that's good.

Manners recognize differences between people. There are certain things people do that say "You're number one" or "Your needs come first." These actions are called *signs of deference,* and to lots of people they symbolize good manners. They're rooted in tradition—and in kindness. Deference turns up in all sorts of ways in manners, but here are a few of the big ones.

Hold doors open for adults. When you and a friend are going through a doorway, let her go ahead of you.

Guests go first. When you're pouring lemonade, pour your friend's glass before you pour your own. When you start a game, let her have the first turn. And when there's only one cookie left? You know who gets it.

Give up your seat on a crowded bus or subway to anybody who looks as if he or she needs to sit down more than you do. This includes older people and people with babies or small children.

Men and women have followed different rules in the past. For many years, men were expected to give all these same signs of deference to women. A polite man opened doors for a woman and let her enter first. He stood when a woman entered a room at a party, and offered her his seat. He walked between a woman and the curb on city streets to protect her from any rain or dirt kicked up by a passing car. Many people keep up these traditions today. Others prefer to see women show their strength and independence by doing these things for themselves.

good impressions

We all know we shouldn't judge a book by its cover, but the fact is that most of us do make judgments about others based on how they look and talk. This is especially true if we're meeting someone for the first time.

Don't let this business of appearances spook you. Instead, try out the tips on these pages. You'll *look* more confident, and that can often make you *feel* more confident. The more you practice these things, the more natural they'll seem. A little work on the outside girl lets the girl inside shine through—and that, of course, is the entire point.

Stand tall

Your body says a lot about what you think of yourself. Hold your head up. Pull your shoulders back. Talk in a strong voice. Walk like a girl who's ready to meet the world, and you'll begin to feel like one. You'll find that others will see you that way, too.

Make eye contact

Look people in the eye. It shows that you're friendly and honest. It also tells others that you're interested in them and in what they're saying.

Say hello

"Hi" means "I know you. I'm glad to see you, even if we're not going to stop and talk." Silence means . . . well, who knows? It might mean "I'm mad at you" or "I don't like you"—or simply "There you are, but so what?"

Use names

Greet people by name. It shows that you care who they are, which makes them feel good.

If you have trouble remembering names, practice saying them when they're fresh in your mind. For instance, if you're introduced to a new girl, say her name right away. (If you didn't quite catch it, ask her to repeat it until you do.) Then use her name several more times before the conversation's done. The more often you use the name today, the better chance you have of remembering it tomorrow.

Shake hands

Step up and shake hands when you're saying hello to an adult, especially if the situation is fairly formal. Offer your right hand (even if you're left-handed) and say the person's name: "Hi, Ms. Puptent." When she puts her hand in yours, clasp it firmly for one quick shake.

choose your words

Manners are all about communication, so put some thought into the words you use to express yourself.

Those **magic words** people have been telling you about all your life really are sort of magic. Say "please" and people cooperate. Say "thank you" and get a smile. These words make everything a little easier and happier—both for others and for you.

Other words are better avoided entirely. **Junk words,** for instance. Words that have nothing to do with the sense of a sentence can be, you know, like, so annoying, like, if you, like, use them constantly, you know? So don't.

Then there are all those **lazy words**—hmm, nah, eh, huh, yeah. We all use them, but overdo it and you'll give the impression that you dragged yourself out of a deep sleep to have this conversation and wish you were still in bed.

Lots of kids use **put-downs** when they're kidding around with their friends. "So what?" "Who cares?" "Shut up." Put-downs are supposed to be funny. Maybe. But a put-down always makes another person feel a bit dumber than she did before you said it. Put-downs sting—maybe a little, maybe a lot.

Keep in mind that **words that work with one kind of person might not work with another.** For instance, you and a close friend may say "duh" just in fun. But if you use "duh" with a kid you don't know well, it's hurtful. And if you use it with an adult, it's insulting.

Swear words: You don't need them. With hundreds of thousands of words to choose from in the English language, why use the ones that were designed to insult and offend people?

Finally, pleasant words don't count if the **tone of your voice** says something entirely different. Yell "I'm sorry," and it means you're not.

respect

It all boils down to respect.

Your manners tell other people that you respect them. Your manners also say that you respect yourself.

You're strong and self-reliant—you don't have to put yourself first. You're in control. You're poised. You know that offering respect to people who are older than you are and people in authority doesn't take away from the respect you have for yourself.

In fact, you know that the more respect you give, the more you get.

In a world with a lot of selfishness, you choose kindness and honor.

Who wouldn't respect a person like that?

let's talk

introductions

It's open house at your new school, and the place is packed. You spot a girl you knew in preschool, a boy from the pool, even your old baby-sitter. So many familiar faces! What do you do when you end up in the library with friends who don't know each other? Introduce them.

Say both names and get things started by offering a little information about each person. There are a few rules about how to do this, but if you forget the rules, it's not the end of the world. The worst mistake is not to make the introduction at all.

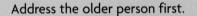

Address the older person first.

Mr. Kander, I'd like to introduce my friend Freddy Ebb.

Freddy, Mr. Kander works with my mom.

Address a woman before a man.

Lynn Fontanne, I'd like to introduce my swim coach, Al Lunt.

Al, Lynn used to babysit for me.

Identify the people you're introducing, and use the names they'll u[se] each other.

> Ms. Evans, I'd like to introduce my cousin, Roy Rogers.

> Roy, Ms. Evans is my neighbor.

An introduction is a good opportunity to let someone know that members of your family use different last names.

> Mom, Dad, I'd like to introduce my friend Sarah Vaughn.

> Sarah, this is my mother, Ms. Rogers, and my father, Mr. Hart.

It's also a good way to identify stepparents.

> Ms. Gilbert, I'd like to introduce my stepfather, Mr. Sullivan.

> Art, Ms. Gilbert is my English teacher.

What if you forget someone's name completely? All is not lost. Introduce the person you do know, and chances are, the other one will finish the job for you by saying her name herself.

> This is Lynn.

> Hi, Lynn, I'm Loretta.

mr., ms., and more

Pop quiz: Your friend's mom is working away in the kitchen when you enter their house. You're a girl with good manners, so the next thing you do is
a. greet her.
b. walk on by as if she were a floor lamp.

Yes, friends, the answer is a.

For reasons scientists have yet to discover, some kids think certain adults are invisible. Not so! Parents enjoy a friendly hello and a big smile as much as you do. So make it a point to greet the adults who cross your path. Use those tried-and-true words "please" and "thank you." Ask these people a question or two about their day, and take a moment or two to answer the questions they ask you. You may be surprised how much you enjoy it.

What do you use?

These days, many kids address adults by their first names. That's fine if the adult has invited you to do it. Until then, you should stick with Mr., Ms., Mrs., or Miss, depending on what the person prefers.

Mr. = a man

Mrs. = a married woman

Ms. = a woman, married or unmarried

Mr. & Ms. = a couple with different last names

Mr. & Mrs. or Mr. & Ms. = a couple with the same last name

Miss = a girl or unmarried woman

"Miss" isn't used as much as it used to be. Many people feel it's inappropriate to identify women by whether or not they're married.

In some parts of the country, particularly the South, many people use "sir" and "ma'am" to show respect.

There are lots of special rules that apply to university professors, politicians, diplomats, royalty, religious leaders, and members of the military. So if you have some VIPs (very important people) in your future, talk to an adult about how to address them.

conversation

Break the ice

You may be shy. You may have nothing to say. But if you stand silently beside another person, how is she to know you're not just unfriendly? Ask some questions: "When did you move in?" "Who's your teacher?" The more she talks, the more relaxed you'll both feel.

Take turns

A conversation is like a tennis match. You say something. The other person takes your thought and bops back one of her own. That's how it goes: back and forth, back and forth. If one or the other holds on to the ball and starts talking nonstop, the game's over.

Listen

We all like a good listener because she makes us feel that our thoughts and feelings matter. If you want to become a better listener:

• Encourage the other person to talk by asking questions.

• Let her know you've heard what she's said by commenting on it.

• Don't always switch the subject back to yourself.

Don't interrupt

Wait till the other person stops talking before you start. If you want to drive somebody crazy, interrupting is a good way to do it.

Zzz

If someone's boring you:

do

- Try to change the subject.

- Make a nice excuse. ("I'd better go to class." "I think I'll get some juice." "Guess I'd better leave now. See you soon!") Then make your escape.

don't

- Let your eyes wander around the room, looking for other people you'd rather be with.

- Say, "Can we change the subject? This is boring."

- Walk off without saying anything.

If you want to **avoid** boring other people:

- Ask them questions.

- Talk about something other than yourself.

- Don't talk all the time.

- Don't tell really long stories, give really long speeches, or describe every little detail of a dream, TV show, or movie.

gossip

Could this be you? Circle your answers.

1. A girl on the bus told Phoebe that Sofia did something incredibly mean to Maya. Is it true? Who knows? Who cares? It's exciting, so you repeat it to Jasmine.

   yes   no

2. "Promise you won't tell?" asks Rachel. "Promise," you reply. But you do tell. It's OK. You made the other person promise not to tell.

   yes   no

3. Everybody's dumping on Madison. She's mean, she's stuck-up, she's two-faced—and she cheated on the English test. You say nothing, though you know it's not true.

   yes   no

4. When the other girls start talking about Daniel, you blurt out Jing's secret: "Jing likes him." Oh, well. What's the big deal about keeping that a secret, anyway?

   yes   no

5. "Emma's dad yells at her all the time," you say. Actually, you heard him yell at her once. And maybe it wasn't so much yelling as talking loud. Still, he was mad.

   yes   no

Answers

If you answered yes, here's what you need to know.

1. Don't repeat what you don't know. Rumors can hurt people—damage their reputations, lose them friends, leave them crying in their rooms late at night. Keeping a rumor alive to amuse yourself is as bad as starting the rumor to begin with. For that matter, even if you do know something is true, it's mean to repeat it if it's going to hurt someone else.

2. The responsibility for keeping a secret you promised to keep belongs to you and you alone. You're kidding yourself if you think you can pass it off to the next person in line. You let it out, and odds are excellent that this third person will treat her promise as lightly as you did yours.

3. Silence in a situation like this amounts to agreeing with something you know is wrong. Speak up with the truth.

4. It's not up to you to decide whether or not a friend's confidence is important. If she asked you not to repeat it, that's all that counts.

5. Rumors grow from half-truths, exaggerations, and plain old ignorance. Be responsible for what you say. Little fibs can morph into huge lies.

nosy questions

When it comes to conversation, there are good questions and there are nosy questions. Good questions lead people to talk about things they want to talk about. Nosy questions embarrass them or make them uncomfortable. Do you know a nosy question when you see one? Find out. Circle the questions that should not have been asked.

1. Nice car, Mr. Addams. How much did it cost?

2. That birdhouse is neat. How long did it take you to make it?

3. Did you grow up in Ottumwa, Mr. Watterson?

4. What's your middle name?

5. How much does your cat weigh?

6. How much do you weigh?

8. Mrs. Steig, do you dye your hair?

7. I heard that your cousin committed suicide. Why did he do it?

9. We could hear your parents fighting last night from next door. What was it about?

10. Your hair sure is white, Mrs. Thurber. Just how old are you?

11. May I see the new kittens, please?

12. Is Garry going to summer camp again, Mrs. Outcault?

13. Why did your dad get fired? Was he bad at his job or something?

14. Why does your brother take those pills?

15. What do your parents keep in there?

16. Is there a bathroom on this floor?

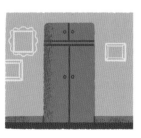

Answers

OK questions: 2, 3, 4, 5, 11, 12, 16

Nosy questions: 1, 6, 7, 8, 9, 10, 13, 14, 15

what do you do?

What to say when you don't know what to say.

Your brother's girlfriend walks in the door. Her hair is red. Yesterday it was blonde—and looked a whole lot better.

An obvious change in someone's appearance is like an elephant in the kitchen—it's just too big to ignore. But if you say what you're thinking, this girl will feel terrible. So make it short and sweet: "You changed your hair! Cool." It's not right to lie, but sometimes it's better to leave a thought unsaid than to hurt someone.

Jenna bursts into tears at lunch. Sobbing, she tells you, "My parents are getting divorced!"

Express your sympathy and concern ("I'm really sorry!"). Offer what help you can ("You can come over to my house anytime"). If Jenna doesn't want to talk, leave her in peace. If she does want to talk, listen. Questions about her future are OK ("Will you still come to this school?"). Prying into her parents' troubles is not OK ("What do they fight about?"). Finally, don't say bad things about either of Jenna's parents—even if she does.

You're visiting your dying Uncle Lev in the hospital. "Hi, Kelcy," he says when you walk in. "How's my girl?" He's got tubes in his arms, he looks horrible, and you wish you were anywhere but here.

Hospital rooms make a lot of people feel like running for the car. Don't do it. Walk on in and say, "I'm doing fine, Uncle Lev. But I'm so sorry you're sick!" Ask questions about his daily comfort: "Are the doctors and nurses nice?" "Is there anything I can get for you?" If Uncle Lev brings up a subject, talk about that. If he doesn't, talk about something going on in your life. Talk about things you've talked about in the past—football, your cousin Jimmy, or teaching your pets tricks. The two of you may laugh—and that's great. Laughter can cheer you both up and help you relax. You may also cry. That's OK, too. It's right to acknowledge powerful feelings and to express fear and love. Stay a half hour or less so that you don't tire him out. Then you can head home with a full heart, knowing you did what you could to comfort your uncle when he needed it most.

"The Hornets play dirty," Mr. Burns says to your dad. You've played the Hornets, and you know this isn't true. Is it OK to speak up and say so?

Absolutely. Say, "Mr. Burns, I don't agree. The Hornets were fine sports when we played them." Express yourself politely, but do express yourself. It's not bad manners to share strong beliefs or opinions—especially when it comes to someone's honor and big issues of right and wrong.

phone basics

One at a time

Having a phone in your hand doesn't mean you can have two conversations at once.

If you're playing a game with your friend Natalie, play the game—don't spend ten minutes sending texts to Ashley while Natalie stares out the window. On the other hand, if you're on the phone with Ashley after dinner, you should be talking to her—not watching TV or typing a message to Natalie. When people are talking to you, they want to know you're really listening. So listen. Have one conversation at a time.

When to call

If it's before nine in the morning or after ten at night, don't. People in the house may be asleep, even if your friend isn't. Avoid calling and texting during the dinner hour, too.

The family phone

Some parents think a simple **"Hello"** is fine for answering the house phone. Others prefer children to answer by identifying the family:

"Hello, this is the Ledbetters' residence."

If the call is for your brother Trent, go find him to tell him. Walk upstairs. Trot downstairs. Do whatever you need to do, but don't stand in the kitchen and holler, **"TRENT, THE PHONE'S FOR YOU! IT'S THAT GIRL AGAIN!"**

Naturally, you should also remember this is a shared line. If your sister is waiting to make a call and you've been chatting with a friend for twenty minutes, it's time to hang up and give her a turn. If your family has call-waiting and the call coming in is more important than the call you're on, tell your friend you'll have to phone her back later.

Talking in a public place

The world does not want to be an audience to your phone call.

You are not in an alternate universe when you're talking on a cell phone. People all around can hear you, whether they like it or not—especially when you crank up the volume of your voice, as many people do.

So be considerate. Find a place away from other people to have your conversation. Go into a different room, find a quiet hallway, or step outside. There is almost always a place you can retreat to. If you can't move—if, say, you're on a bus or in a car—then keep the conversation short and talk in a normal voice.

Obviously, the ringer should be off in movies, at performances, and in school (if phones are even allowed)—anyplace where the noise would disturb what's going on. When the event begins, check the phone to be sure it's off. Turn the ringer off in restaurants, too. You can always put the phone on vibrate. If someone calls and you absolutely must talk, slip outside to do it.

Know when to stop

You're enthusiastic and have a lot to say, and that's great. But don't keep a friend on the phone for an hour and then follow it up with twenty text messages. It's just too much. You'll tire her out.

Eating on the phone

Don't. It's gross.

Messages

If you're leaving a voice message, keep it short. It's a message, not a conversation. Give your name and phone number, indicate the time, and briefly explain why you're calling: "Hi. This is Jenny Lind. I'm calling for Sarah about the picnic. It's 7 p.m. Sarah, would you call me back, please? Thanks."

If you're taking a message for someone else, write everything down while the caller is still on the line. Don't be afraid to ask a caller to go slowly, repeat things, or spell a name. You're being careful, and the person receiving the message will appreciate that.

If you're home alone and a caller asks for one of your parents, don't say you're by yourself. Instead say, "I'm sorry. Mom can't come to the phone right now. May I take a message?"

Wrong numbers

If you call a wrong number, say, "I'm sorry. I think I have the wrong number." Don't just hang up—it's rude. Check to see what numbers you dialed the first time before you dial again, so that if you have the information written down incorrectly, you won't dial a wrong number twice.

If you answer the phone and someone has dialed a wrong number, be polite about the mistake. Remember, though, that it's unsafe to give out your name or any other information. If the caller tries to start any kind of conversation, hang up.

Keeping in touch

If you've got a cell phone, use it the way your parents intend for you to use it. If they want you to stay in touch with them, do so. Keep the phone charged. Take it with you when you go places. Call in to let your mom and dad know where you are, and call or text in again if your plans change or you go someplace different. Needless to say, answer your phone if they call.

being online

☺ i lv nstant misengring nd eemial dton u?

Well, sure. And writing in computer shorthand is fun, too.

But keep in mind that another person is actually going to have to read what you write. The message doesn't have to have perfect spelling and punctuation, like a paper for school, but if you send something so full of mistakes that a person has to struggle to read it, you're saying, "I can't be bothered. You do the work."

☺ I GET IT.
ANYTHING ELSE?

Yep. Don't type your words in all capital letters. It seems as if you're yelling.

☺ Here's something I've wondered about. Do I have to respond to every single e-mail or message I get?

No. If you did, nobody could ever get up from a computer. But if somebody's put a lot of time into an e-mail or asks specific questions, then you should respond.

If a person is bombarding you with e-mails, and you just can't keep up, say so: "It's fun to send messages, but I'm spending too much time on the computer and have to cut back." Of course, it's also good to keep this in mind when you send messages. You don't want to become a pest by flooding a friend's inbox and demanding attention.

☺ How about forwarding e-mails? Can I do that?

A message sent to you is meant for you. You should no more hand it around than you would hand around a letter. It's a violation of the writer's privacy, not to mention her trust in you. There are exceptions: If a friend sent you the soccer schedule or the URL for a funny website, you can forward that. But a personal message—no.

☺ My friend likes to pretend she's someone else when she's online. She makes up stuff. She says it's fun and doesn't hurt anybody.

Not so. Lying is lying. If you engage someone in a false conversation, you're playing her for a fool. Nobody wants that, including you. And remember that pretending online isn't always just for "fun"—see page 92 for safety tips.

☺ My friends and I seem to get into more fights when we write one another.

No surprise there. People tend to dash off messages on a computer saying things that they would never say face-to-face. Make it a habit to reread a message before you send it. Use that time to think about how it's going to sound to the other person. If you're talking about a touchy subject, read it twice. Would you tell that friend the same thing if she were standing in the room beside you? Are you going to be sorry tomorrow you sent this message? You're still you when you're online. You're just as responsible for what you say on-screen as you are for what you say anyplace else.

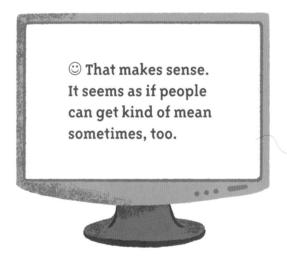

☺ That makes sense. It seems as if people can get kind of mean sometimes, too.

They sure can. Girls can gang up on other girls online in truly horrible ways. (Boys can, too!) They will say hurtful things. They will block another girl from games or groups. They will post embarrassing pictures. They will fuel ugly rumors. Being the victim of all this is awful. Would the tormentors describe themselves as "bullies"? Probably not. Bullies always have trouble recognizing themselves in the mirror. But that's what they are. Trashing someone online is cruel and vicious. You want no part of it.

hosts & guests

at a friend's

You're getting together with a friend. Sounds fun! If she's coming to your place, make her feel welcome and comfortable. If you're going to hers, be respectful of property and privacy. It's all part of being a good host and a good guest—and a thoughtful and considerate friend.

Being a host

Greet your guest at the door. Show her where to hang up her coat and stash her belongings. If she's never been to your home before, show her around and introduce her to your family.

Is there any special information your friend needs to know? Is the dog friendly? Is your mom's office off-limits? Clue her in so that she'll know what to do—and what not to do.

Ask your guest if she'd like something to eat and drink. It's a good way to make her feel welcome.

Be flexible when choosing what to do. Suggest several different activities and ask your friend for her suggestions, too. Pick something you're both happy with.

See your guest to the door when she leaves. If your parents are driving her home, go along in the car.

Being a guest

If your shoes are wet or dirty, take them off when you come in the door. Don't dump your coat and belongings in a heap on the floor or on a chair.

Be friendly to other people in the house. Greet them by name.

Don't wander around the house on your own. Stick with your friend and let her be the guide.

It's up to the host to offer food and drink. If you know your host well, it's OK to let her know you're hungry, but you should never help yourself.

Respect the belongings of the people in the house. Don't examine or use objects as if they were your own.

If you need to use a phone or anything else that doesn't belong to you, ask first.

If you helped make a mess, be sure you help clean it up.

Say thank you when you leave.

sleepovers

Every household has its own habits and routines. When you're invited to a sleepover, your job is to fit in and pitch in.

At dinner, use good table manners and clear your place when you've finished eating. Help out in the kitchen and with any other chores your friend has to do.

Snooping is wrong. Don't open up drawers in a desk or dresser. Don't inspect cupboards and closets. Never, ever read diaries, letters, bills, or other papers—even if they're lying out on a counter or desktop.

Be quiet late at night. A girl who keeps sleepy people up at 2 a.m. is a girl who probably won't be invited back anytime soon.

That said, if you're ill, homesick, or scared, it's OK to turn to your friend or her parents for help. Manners don't require you to pretend you're all right when you're not.

The bathroom is a private place. If you want to be alone when you change clothes, that's the place to do it. Just don't stay in there too long, and be sure it's clean when you leave. Use only the towel you're told to use. Rinse the sink out after you've brushed your teeth, and wipe up any water on the countertop. When you've finished, fold your towel and hang it up.

Before you say good-bye, make sure you've made your bed or stripped it. And remember to thank your friend and her parents when you leave.

invitations

Invitations should be sent at least ten days before the party. Be sure to tell your guests everything they need to know.

When and where will the party take place?

What sort of party is it?

Who's giving the party? (You, of course!)

IT'S A SUMMER BIRTHDAY SPLASH

WHO
Wendy Waters

WHEN
Saturday, July 14
11:30 - 2:00

WHERE
Lakewood Public Pool

R.S.V.P. (234-5678)

Bring a towel and swimsuit

Is there any **special info** your guests should know?

R.S.V.P. is short for the French phrase *Répondez s'il vous plaît* (reh-pon-day seel voo play). It means **"Reply,** if you please." A guest who receives an invitation saying R.S.V.P. should tell the host as soon as possible whether or not she can come.

what do you do?

What do you do if you see someone handing out invitations and she doesn't give one to you?
Very Hurt

Invitations should be mailed, e-mailed, or delivered to homes, not handed out at school in front of girls who aren't invited. When you're left out in this inconsiderate way, you may be tempted to confront the host and ask, "Why didn't you ask me?" or "Can I please come anyway?" Don't. It will only make you feel worse. Instead, find a friend. Talking and laughing with another girl can help you hide your embarrassment and soothe hurt feelings. Remind yourself that the person who's done something she should be ashamed of is the host—not you.

Once a girl invited me to her birthday party. When my birthday came around, I could invite only three people. I picked my three closest friends, and she was not one of them. She was very upset. I felt so bad. Was that the right thing to do?
Confused

When a friend invites you to her birthday party, it's nice to return the favor by inviting her to yours. But if you've been to a lot of birthday parties and can have only three guests to yours, you'll need to find other ways to express your friendship. If you know you're going to leave a friend out, invite her to a movie or a sleepover on another day. Honesty is a good idea, too. Getting left out is never fun, but if a girl knows that your mom set a limit on guests, the news might be a whole lot easier to take.

I invited this girl to a party. Now another girl says she won't come if that girl does. What should I do?
In the Middle

Tell the girl who's threatening to skip your party that you aren't going to change your guest list for her. A good guest tries to get along with other guests whether she likes them or not. And she doesn't bully the host, either.

I planned a party and all twelve people said they could come, but only nine showed up.
Erika

For every girl who doesn't show up when she says she will, there's an empty chair and a hurt friend wondering *Where can she be?* You have every right to be annoyed with these girls and to say, "I'm disappointed you didn't come to the party" when you see them next. If they don't apologize nicely or offer a good excuse, it may be time to start looking for some new friends.

One of my best friends is having a party. I'm sure that I should be invited, but I never got an invitation.
Left Out

Option 1: Wait and see. If you're really invited, your friend may bring up the party in conversation, and it will be easy to tell her your invitation never came. **Option 2:** If other girls are talking about the party, tell them you didn't get an invitation. Word may get back to the host. **Option 3:** Ask your friend straight out, "Am I invited?" But before you do, think carefully about what you'll say if she says no.

I wasn't planning to invite a certain friend to my birthday party, but she kept calling me and asking when my party was. I had no choice but to invite her.
Harassed Hostess

It was nice of you to include this girl, but in cases like this it's also OK to say, "I'm sorry I wasn't able to invite you to this party." The friend may get angry—disappointed people often do. But as long as you hold on to your own temper and say what you can to heal hurt feelings, you're in the right. You owe the caller kindness, politeness, and respect. You don't owe her an invitation.

party pitfalls

Parties can celebrate friendships. They can also destroy them. How good are you at avoiding disaster? Answer these questions and find out.

1. The pizzas arrive, and Amanda and Taylor start fighting again.

  a. You take a slice of pizza and listen.

  b. You take sides and join in: "Oh, yes, you did—"

  c. You say, "Amanda, Taylor, your fighting is wrecking my party. Please stop."

2. You've had a snack, and now, as the invitations said, you're all playing basketball. "No way," says Justine. "I hate basketball. I want to go skating outside."

  a. You say, "OK. Skating it is."

  b. You yell, "Don't be a jerk. It's my party, and we're going to do what I want."

  c. You say, "I want to play basketball as planned. Maybe we can skate outside later."

3. Lily is totally out of control. She's slamming into other people on her skates and upsetting everyone.

    a. You take off your skates and cry. It's hopeless.

    b. You push Lily into a bush. Ha! Serves her right.

    c. You say, "Lily, you're hurting people. Please stop being so crazy."

4. You're in your sleeping bags and angry voices rise. Yep, it's Amanda and Taylor—at it again.

    a. You pull the covers over your head and wish you'd never had this party.

    b. You scream, "Stop it, stop it, stop it!" till the cat hides under the sofa. Then you burst into tears.

    c. You go get your mom. It's time for an adult to step in and call a halt.

Answers

Doormat

If you checked mostly a's, you let rude guests take over. Don't. A guest is supposed to arrive in good spirits, ready to do whatever she can to make the party a success. She's in the wrong if she fights, tries to run the show, or gets so wild that others can't have fun. When you have a guest like this, stand up for yourself and tell her to stop. You'll have more fun—and so will the other girls at your party.

Hothead

If you checked mostly b's, you need to work on controlling your temper. Problem guests can be frustrating, but what happens if you blow up? The fight gets bigger, louder, and meaner. Your party veers out of control and into a ditch.

Diplomat

If you checked mostly c's, you keep your cool when guests act up. You don't get involved in silly fights. You stand back and tell your friends, in an honest, direct way, that they're out of line. This is the best chance you have for reminding a friend that she's making a mess of your party. And if that doesn't work, you know it's time to call in the adults. 51

Quiz

Are you a horrid host? Could this be you? No—or yes?

1. You have eight guests—and two best friends. At dinner you say, "Amber and Danielle, sit next to me!" Before the game you cry, "Amber and Danielle are on my team." At bedtime you whisper, "Amber! Danielle! Put your sleeping bags by mine."

yes   no

2. Nadya shows up without a gift. She says she forgot it. Forgot it?!? You let her know what you think of *that* excuse!

yes   no

3. It's your party, and that means you're in charge. Every girl is going to do exactly what you tell her to do, exactly when you tell her to do it. Do your guests have suggestions? Too bad! You're in charge here.

yes   no

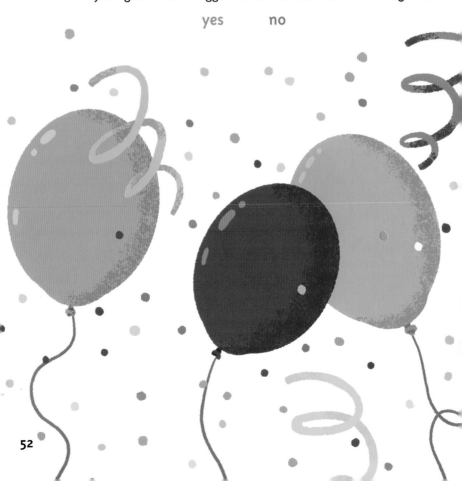

4. New walkie-talkies! You hand one to Amber, and the two of you have a great time whispering from different rooms. When the other girls say they're feeling bored and left out, you reply, "It's not my fault walkie-talkies are meant for two."

yes   no

5. Your mom made you invite Paige—and you've made sure all your other friends know that. Now you don't hesitate to join in the laughter when one of your real friends makes an itty-bitty comment about Paige's hair. What's the problem? You're all just teasing.

yes   no

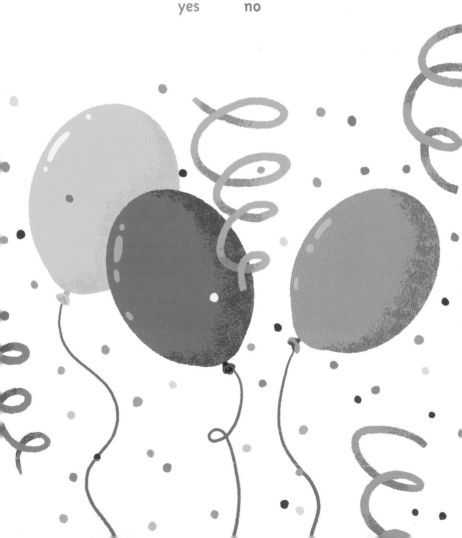

Answers

If you said **yes** even once, you're in need of a manners makeover.

1. Playing favorites is insulting to every girl who's left out.

2. Gifts are given in friendship—not forked over as payment for an invitation. A girl shouldn't criticize a gift. She shouldn't demand one, either.

3. Don't be a dictator. Yes, you've got plans for your party, and yes, your friends should go along. But if you try to control every single little thing they do, no one's going to have fun.

4. Activities at a party should include everybody. Period.

5. A host is responsible for the well-being of every guest. At the first sign of any teasing or petty meanness, she should speak out: "Leave her alone. That's not nice." A girl who picks on one of her own guests earns the title of "most horrible host."

boy-girl parties

Q: **How do I know what to wear?**

A: Figure it out the way you always do—talk to the host or call other girls who are going to the party to see what they're planning to wear. Then go to your closet and pull out something that makes you feel good.

Q: **What if I get to a party and there's no parent home?**

A: There should always be a parent or some other adult in the house during a party, and this is especially true for a boy-girl party. An adult's presence ensures that things don't get too wild. If you realize that you kids have the house to yourselves, tell your host that your parents don't allow you to go to unsupervised parties, call home, and arrange to get picked up.

Q: **Can I ask a boy to dance?**

A: Sure.

Q: What if a boy asks me to dance?

A: Do you want to? Then say yes, stand up, and go do it. If you're nervous about your dancing, make some jokes about it. Chances are, the boy will say he's worried about looking like a sick emu, too. You can get over your nerves together.

If you're so nervous that you don't want to dance at all, it's OK to say no: "Sorry, I'm going to sit the dancing out." Maybe this boy would like to hang out at the snack table with you instead.

Q: But what if I like to dance but I just don't want to dance with this particular boy?

A: You can say, "No thanks, I'm tired." But if you do that, you can't accept a different boy's invitation two seconds later.

Q: But what if I really, really like the second boy, and I really, really don't like the first one?

A: Doesn't matter. The boy you reject may be the last boy in the world that you want to dance with, but he was nice enough to ask you to dance and deserves kindness and respect in return. The absolute worst thing you can do is make fun of a boy who made himself vulnerable by extending this invitation to you.

Q: And if nobody asks me to dance at all?

A: Get a bunch of girls together, find some floor, and dance in a group. Kids do it all the time. It's fun—sometimes more fun than dancing with a single partner.

Q: What if everybody wants to play Spin the Bottle or Truth or Dare, and I don't want to?

A: Say so: "No, thanks. I don't want to play." If somebody gives you grief, say, "What's the big deal? I don't want to. It's my choice. Why should that matter to you?" Give yourself something else to do. Take charge of the music or pull a game off the shelf. There are probably other people who are uncomfortable with this situation, and now that you've had the nerve to speak up, they might join you.

Q: And if I just get uncomfortable and want to go home?

A: Make a polite excuse and go. Manners don't require that you stay in a situation that feels bad.

gifts

presents

Gifts are a way of showing you care about another person. They're great to give and great to get.

Giving

Invitations to birthday parties, weddings, and bridal or baby showers call for gifts. The exception is when the host has written "No gifts, please" on the invitation. Gifts are also a tradition for various religious holidays, including Christmas and Hanukkah.

Wrap your gift neatly and tape a card on top, with your name and the name of the recipient. A greeting, even a simple "Happy Birthday," is nice, too.

Receiving

When you get a gift, thank the giver warmly: "Great! I'll really use this!" "How pretty!" **"It's my favorite color."** If you can't find something nice to say about the gift, say something nice about the giver: "How thoughtful of you! Thank you so much!"

Sometimes you'll get a gift similar to something you already have. In that case, say thank you as you always do but talk with your parents later. If the gift came from a relative, your folks may say it's OK to tell the giver it's a duplicate. Most people would rather have you exchange a gift than have it end up in the bottom of a drawer. Also, see if the gift has a tag that tells you where it came from. Many stores will make exchanges without a receipt.

Always write a thank-you note.

what do you do?

Should I shop for my family myself? I have always let my parents buy something and just say on the tag that it's from me, but I'm not so sure that it's right since I'm older now.
Ashley

If you have enough money to buy things for yourself—treats, books, clothes, accessories—then the answer is yes. It's probably time that you start saving some of your allowance and other earnings to spend on gifts for the people in your immediate family. A gift that you picked out and paid for yourself will mean ten times more to the person who gets it—and ten times more to you. The gifts don't have to be fancy. In fact, you could decide to make something and spend your money on materials. Handmade gifts are often the most wonderful gifts of all.

How much should I spend on friends' birthday gifts? I don't want people to think I don't have money, but I don't want to be broke, either.
Puzzled

Ideally, you'd spend roughly the same amount on your friends as they spend on you. So think about three gifts you got from friends for your last birthday. Look in the stores to see how much they cost. Figure out an average amount, and make that your budget when you shop. What about wealthy friends who spent more on you than you can afford? It's OK to spend an average amount on them, too.

One time a friend gave me the most adorable little teddy bear as a Christmas present. This came as a surprise, and I had no gift for her in return. I made the day, though, by saying lots of thank-yous and taking the bear with me everywhere!
Allison

Clever you! When you're caught empty-handed, it's even more important than usual to let the giver know that you appreciate the gift. Follow that up with a nice thank-you note—and maybe even an invitation to do something special—and you're telling your friend what she needs to know: You don't take her for granted. You care about her and are grateful for her kindness.

thank-yous

A gift requires a thank-you note. An e-mail thank-you might be OK in some situations, but a handwritten note is always better. Writing notes may seem like an ordeal, especially right after your birthday or a big holiday, but silence shows ingratitude. Luckily, writing a nice thank-you is easy. It can even be fun.

Paper

Start with a fresh piece of paper or stationery. Has the dog been chewing on the notepad? Is there a grocery list on the back? Use something else.

Talk

Talk about the gift for several sentences. Have you used it? Did someone else comment on it? Are there things about it that you particularly like?

Ask

Ask some questions about the person to whom you're writing. What's going on at her house? Show that you care about her.

Report

What's the news at your home? Bring Aunt Margo up to date on a thing or two.

Neatness and accuracy

Write carefully. Reread what you've written. Sloppy handwriting and misspelled words tell Aunt Margo, "Boy, I can't wait to get this note over with."

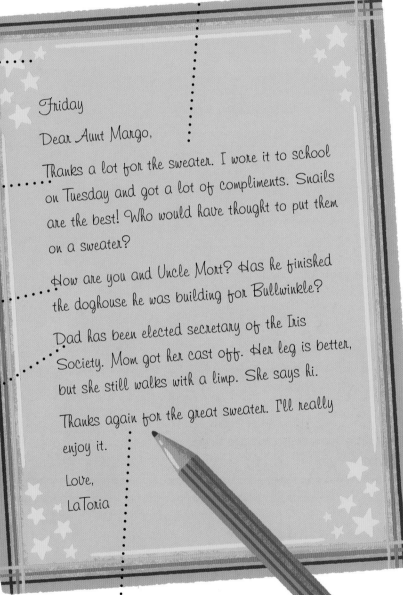

Friday

Dear Aunt Margo,

Thanks a lot for the sweater. I wore it to school on Tuesday and got a lot of compliments. Snails are the best! Who would have thought to put them on a sweater?

How are you and Uncle Mort? Has he finished the doghouse he was building for Bullwinkle?

Dad has been elected secretary of the Iris Society. Mom got her cast off. Her leg is better, but she still walks with a limp. She says hi.

Thanks again for the great sweater. I'll really enjoy it.

Love,
LaToria

Say thanks again

Mention the gift a second time, just before you end.

what do you do?

It's a lot easier to say thank you in an e-mail than it is to say thank you in a note. There's nothing wrong with using a computer, is there?
Ruby

It depends. Sending a nice thank-you electronically can be a fine way to thank a friend or a cousin who goes online frequently—assuming that it's a real letter, not a sentence that you dash off in ten seconds. But this is a casual way to thank people. With someone you don't know as well or with an adult, it's better to write a note and send it through the mail. This is especially true if the gift is very generous or if the giver spent a lot of time making it for you. A traditional thank-you simply carries more clout than a message on a machine. It's more personal and more gracious, so it means more.

Do you always have to write your thank-yous? How about saying thank you when you see people, or calling them on the phone? This way you can tell them more than you could on a piece of paper.
Jill

Saying thank you on the phone is a great idea, but can it replace a written thank-you? For people outside your family, no. Even if your friends are sitting around you when you're opening gifts at a birthday party, it's best to follow up that hurried spoken thank-you with a note. As for gifts from family members, traditions vary. In some families, if you have the chance to say thanks in person or call to say thanks on the phone, that's enough. In others, thank-yous are exchanged as faithfully as gifts. There's one rule you can count on: it's better to write the note than to skip it.

Is it polite to send the same thank-you card to everyone and just fill the person's name in the blank?
Lucy

No. A fill-in-the-blank thank-you makes the person who gets it feel like a fill-in-the-blank friend. It's far better to write a real note to everyone. You can repeat some sentences from one note to the next, but you should also have some lines that are specially written for this gift and this giver.

If I give someone a gift and she doesn't say thank you or even smile at me, how should I feel? I'm upset that I've disappointed her.
Tracey

A gift is a way of showing affection for another person. Does the person who gets a gift EVER have the right to turn up her nose at that? No. If you give a gift you think a friend would like, you've done your part. So how should you feel if your friend is ungrateful? Disappointed in *her*.

Do you always have to send a thank-you note? If someone gives you a candy cane, do you send her a thank-you?
Just Wondering

Presents always deserve a thank-you note. The question is, if somebody hands you a candy cane, is that really a present? Well, yes and no. If the item you're given is inexpensive, unwrapped, and given to you casually, then a warm, spoken "Thank you!" may be enough. If you have any doubt about whether a written thank-you is called for, ask your mom or dad.

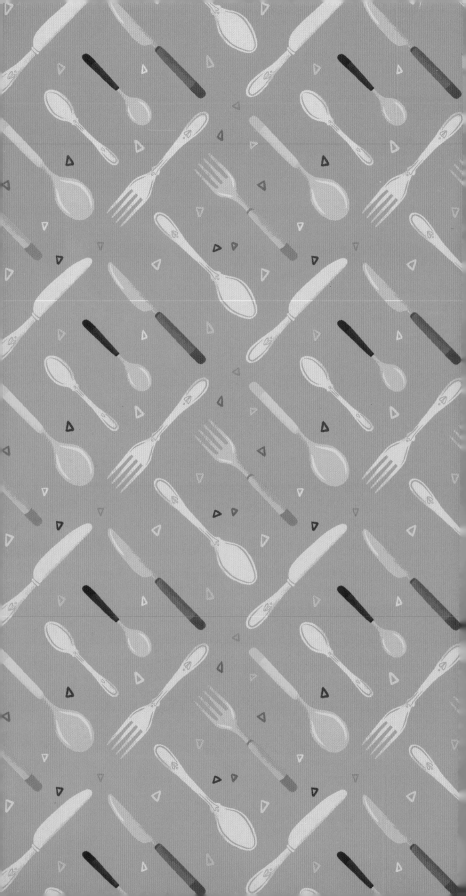

eating

table manners

People need more than good food to enjoy a meal. They also need good company. That's where table manners come in. Table manners remind us how to share and how to be considerate—not to mention how to avoid grossing other people out. They make mealtimes more pleasant at home and are one of the first things people will notice about you when you're a guest.

Help out

Stick your nose in the kitchen before dinner and ask the cook if there's anything you can do to help. Pour drinks, get out the butter, or set the table. A simple place setting looks like this, with the knife blade turned toward the plate.

Wait to begin

Come when you're called. Sit down and put your napkin in your lap but don't start digging into the biscuits until everyone else is seated, too—including the cook. If you're a guest, tradition says to wait for the hostess to take a bite of food. Then you can begin as well.

Get in the spirit

Ditch the electronics. No phone calls, no texting, no computers, no tablets, no TV. Pay attention to the people sitting around you instead. Talk. Tell a story or two about your day. Ask a few questions. How did volleyball practice go for your brother? Did your mom see another coyote on her way to work? Has everybody heard about the Trojan horse the art teacher is building for Greek Week at school? See what kind of conversation you can get going.

Cutting your meat

Hold your knife and fork like this:

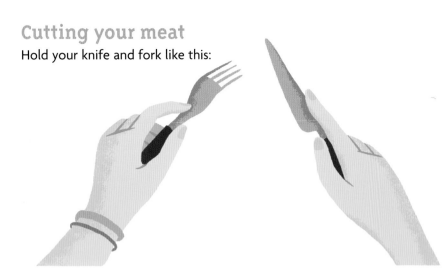

(Don't hold them in your fists.) **Cut one small piece at a time.**
Transfer your fork back to your right hand (if you're right-handed) and
set your knife on the plate as you eat.

Directing traffic

Food is passed to the right. If serving dishes are going both right and
left, they're going to collide like cars on a one-way street. At posh
parties and restaurants, waiters serve from the right and pick up used
dishes from the left.

Helping yourself

Take the portion nearest you.
Leave the utensils neatly together,
handles out, so that the next person
doesn't have to fish through the sauce
to get to them. If it's a big dish, help
the next person by holding it while
he serves himself.

Second helpings

At home, once everybody has been served, it's OK to ask for second
helpings. If you're a guest in someone else's home, however, you should
hold off. If there's enough food for seconds, the hosts will offer it.

Reaching

If for some reason a dish didn't get to you, ask for it: "Please pass the
rolls." If you reach across the table, your elbow may end up in your
pa's peas.

Chewing

Squishy sounds + the sight of chewed-up food
=
disgusting.

That's why you should **chew with your mouth closed** and avoid talking while you're doing it.

At rest

If you've stopped eating for a minute, position your silverware like this:

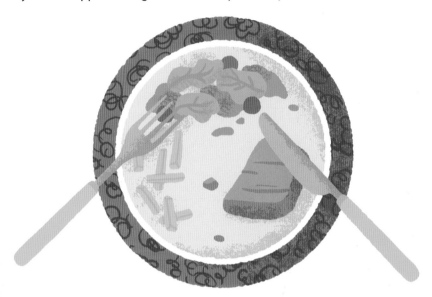

At a restaurant or fancy dinner, this tells the server that you've paused but you're not finished.

Elbows

So why do you have to keep your elbows off the table, anyway? Because slouching over your plate makes you look lazy and bored.

Acting goofy

Blowing bubbles in your milk or making a castle of your mashed potatoes tells the cook you'd rather play with the food than eat it. Does the cook appreciate this? Nope.

what do you do?

It's a happy girl who knows how to handle all kinds of eating situations.

There are anchovies in the salad, and as far as you're concerned, anchovies are the yuckiest things on the planet.

It's OK to eat around bits of food you dislike, as long as you don't sort your food into little piles as you do it. And what if a platter comes along with food you don't want? Pleasantly say, "No, thank you."

Ping! Your fork hits the floor.

Leave the fork on the floor if you're in a restaurant, and ask the server for a new one. If you're at a friend's, pick up the fork and say, "Excuse me, I dropped my fork." That's the host's cue to get you a clean one.

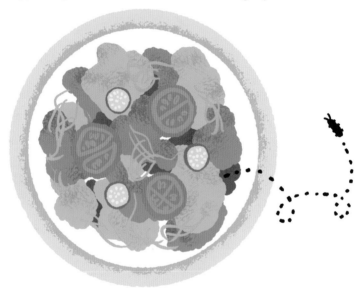

You poke your salad and a bug crawls out.

Say, "May I have another salad?" Explain why if the host asks. Try —really try—not to squeal and make a fuss.

A piece of spinach is wedged between your teeth.

Say, "May I be excused for a moment, please?" Go to the bathroom and do whatever you need to do to get the spinach out. (If you see something stuck in your friend's teeth, don't sit there wondering when she'll notice it herself. Let her know with a small hand motion.)

Your milk topples over onto the tablecloth.

Say, "I'm sorry!" and help clean up. Accidents happen to everybody —including adults.

The moment the host has filled your plate, you realize that you really, really have to go to the bathroom.

Say, "May I be excused for a moment, please?"

There's a UFO on your plate—an Unidentified Food Object. What is it? How do you eat it? You have no idea!

Keep chatting. Wait to see what the hostess does with the UFO on her plate.

You took a bite of meat five minutes ago and are still chewing, trying to get rid of the gristle.

Quietly take the gristle out of your mouth with your thumb and forefinger and place it on the edge of your plate.

The host appears with a platter of deviled eggs, and you're allergic to eggs.

Say, "No, thank you. I'm allergic to eggs." Make a meal of the other foods on the table.

fancy dinners

Going to a formal dinner? Lucky you! At elegant meals, the food isn't served all at once. Instead, foods are brought out, you eat them, and then that plate's removed and replaced with something else. Each part of the dinner is called a *course*. An extremely fancy dinner can have five courses or more—and a menu that lists them. Don't take huge portions, but do try everything. (It's OK if you don't eat everything on your plate.)

MENU

First course is usually a soup or an appetizer.

Second course might be seafood.

Third course is the main dish, or *entrée* (ON-tray), and the vegetables that go with it.

Salad may be served either before or after the main course.

Dessert. Enough said. Yum!

Surprise! **Sweets,** such as chocolate candies, can follow dessert.

Fancy place settings

Each course requires its own silverware. In fact, there are special pieces of silverware designed for special courses (fish knives, oyster forks—the list goes on). Depending on what's being served, a fancy place setting might look something like this:

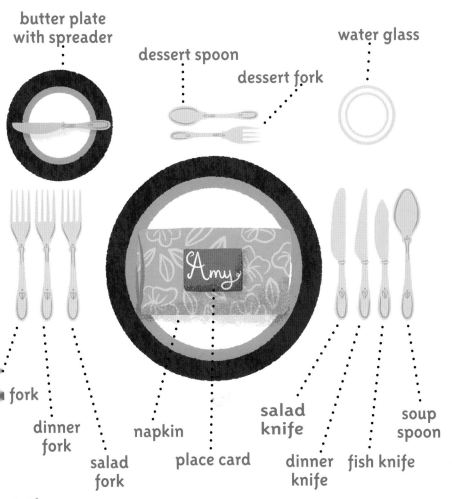

butter plate with spreader

dessert spoon

dessert fork

water glass

fork

dinner fork

salad fork

napkin

place card

salad knife

dinner knife

fish knife

soup spoon

A tip

Even more silverware may appear from the kitchen as the meal goes on. It can get confusing, but follow what the host is doing, and remember this little secret: **the silverware for the food that's served first is placed farthest from the plate.** So no matter how many forks are lined up, relax. All you need to do is pick the one on the outside.

restaurants

No microwave burritos tonight. No home cooking, either. You brush your hair and put on your favorite sweater. You, my dear, are eating out.

Arriving

In a nice restaurant, diners are led to their tables by a hostess or *maître d'* (MAY-truh DEE)—a French term for headwaiter. You're on parade in front of the other diners, **so stand tall and walk briskly.** It's not a good time to fight with your sister about who gets which seat.

Ordering

Perhaps you don't see anything you want on the menu. Look again. Can you find some plain chicken? A simple pasta? Restaurants serve only what's on the menu, so **a wise girl is flexible** when she walks in the door.

When it's your turn to speak, the waitress will look at you. Look back and **talk clearly,** so she knows you want the sherbet and not the sheep brains.

Tabletops

You're in charge of eating your food. The waitstaff is in charge of the tabletop. **Don't rearrange things.** If somebody's going to play with the candle, be sure it's not you.

Traffic

Those trays waiters carry are as heavy and tippy as they look, so **don't block the path between tables** on your way to check out the fish tank.

Noise

Each table is supposed to **be an island.** Nothing going on at one table should affect what's going on at the next. Cell phones should be off or set to vibrate. If you have to make or take a call, take the phone outside or into some private place. And it's nix on loud talking, loud laughing, bumping chairs, and flying sugar packets.

Tipping

In most situations, a customer is expected to leave a little extra money on the table for the waiter or waitress. Fifteen to twenty percent of the total bill is standard.

finger food

The list of foods you shouldn't pick up is pretty long and pretty obvious. (When's the last time you wondered if you could hold your lasagna?) But there are other foods that you may be unsure how best to handle.

Appetizers

Appetizers are **little snacks** served before guests begin the meal. Usually you pluck them off a platter with your fingers or a toothpick, using a napkin for a plate. Some appetizers sit on tiny fluted papers. If so, take the paper with the food. If you need utensils, there will be some nearby on the table.

Dips and chips may also appear. All these things are meant to be shared, which is why a good guest won't re-dip a chip that's already been in her mouth. Nor will she eat all the shrimp balls—sigh!—no matter how much she loves them.

Part of your job as a nibbler is keeping the platter looking nice. This means taking care of your **trash.** Often there is a second plate or bowl near the appetizer tray to hold used toothpicks, shrimp shells, olive pits, radish stubs, papers, or whatever else you might wind up with. If there isn't such a dish, keep your trash in the napkin in your hand until you find a wastebasket. Can you "forget" the napkin on a table or park it in a potted plant? Don't even think about it.

Asparagus

Believe it or not, asparagus may be eaten with the fingers if it's firm. If it's limp and dripping with sauce, go for your fork.

Bananas, bacon, and pickles

At home, you can eat these foods with your fingers. If you're in a fancy setting, use a knife and fork.

Fried chicken

When it comes to fried chicken, do as the hostess is doing. If she picks up her drumstick, you can pick up yours. If she uses her knife and fork, you should do the same.

Tortillas

Use your hands to start, and then switch to your fork to get the good stuff that fell off onto your plate.

Watermelon

If it's cubed, use your fork. If it's sliced, chances are good you're on a picnic, in which case you're free to pick it up. (Just check with your mom before you start spitting seeds at your little sister.)

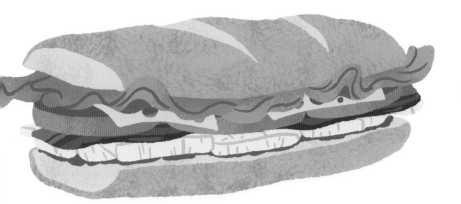

Go ahead

The following foods are finger food no matter where you find them: artichokes, grapes, hamburgers, hot dogs, pizza, and sandwiches.

problem foods

Soup

Insert your spoon at the edge of the bowl closest to you, and move the spoon away from you as you scoop up your soup. If you rest between sips, park the spoon on the soup plate, not in the bowl. Don't **slurp.**

Peas

Use your knife—not your fingers—to get peas and other runaway foods onto your fork. You can also push them up against a backstop, such as a baked potato, until they **roll** onto your fork.

Lobster

A whole lobster is served with a nutcracker. Use the nutcracker to break open the shell, and then **dig** out the meat with a pick or little fork.

Salad

Cut the lettuce into small pieces before you try to eat it. Jamming big leaves into your mouth works, but it isn't pretty. And watch out for small tomatoes. If you eat them whole, they **squirt.**

Spaghetti

Wind spaghetti onto your fork like a ball of string. Stop before you get too much. (A few strands are all you need.)

Bread and rolls

Your roll goes on the little plate to the left of your dinner plate. Break off one bite at a time. What do you use to **spread** the butter? Why, that cute little butter spreader on your bread plate, of course.

Shish kebabs

Take the blunt end of the skewer in one hand and your fork in the other. Point the tip of the skewer downward, and use your fork to **slide** the meat and vegetables onto your plate one chunk at a time.

finished

All done? There are just a few more things to keep in mind.

Leave your silverware positioned like this. →
At a restaurant or a nice dinner, this says
to the waiter, "You can take my plate.
I'm done."

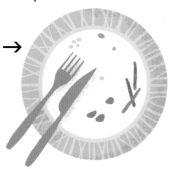

Ask if you may be excused. Thank the cook and say something
nice about the food.

Fold your napkin and put it back on the table.

Push in your chair as you leave the table.

Take your plate to the sink if you're home or at a friend's. Then pitch
in and help clean up.

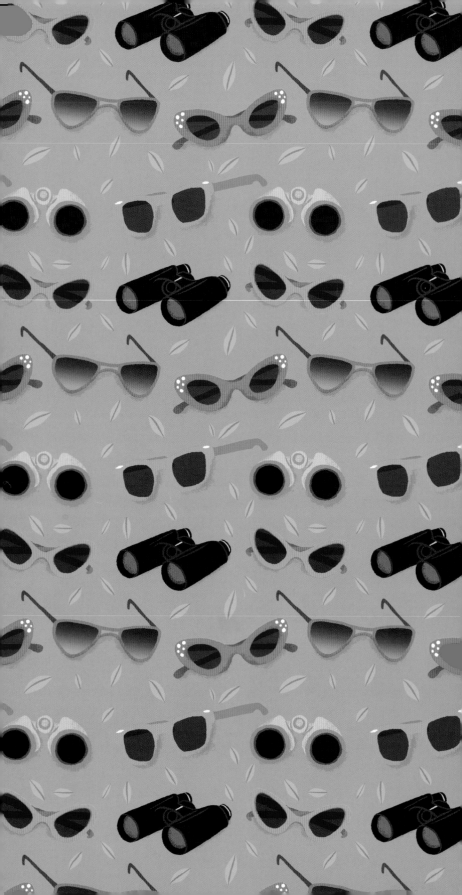

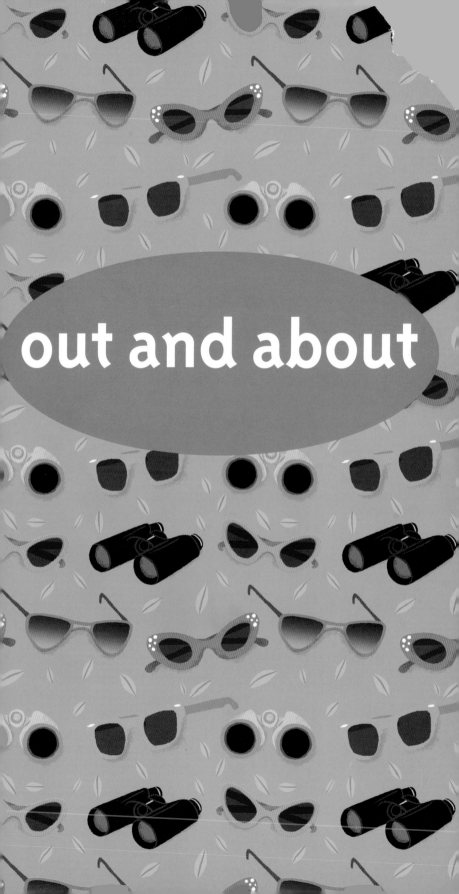

out and about

neighborhoods

No matter where you live, you're part of a community. In fact, you're part of a lot of communities: a neighborhood, a city, a state, a country, a world. You have manners you use with people you know and care for. When you leave your home, take them with you.

1. You know how you feel when your sister leaves a mess for you to clean up. Bear that in mind when you're walking the dog or deciding what to do with an empty soda can. **Pick up after your pet, and hold on to all trash until you find a trash can.**

2. It may be OK to cross the Frabbles' yard on the way to school, but it's not OK to play there as if it were your own. **Respect others' territory.**

3. BOOM-da-BOOM-da-BOOM. You may love that music, but there's simply **no way for you to listen to it loud** without making your neighbors listen to it, too.

4. You may hardly notice your bike tracks on Mr. Ott's lawn, but he may notice them—a lot. The rule is: **if something is going to hurt your neighbor's property in any way, don't do it.**

5. Good neighbors pitch in. Help old Mr. Prunepit drag his trash to the curb. Do some peer tutoring and help little Sara Spigot learn to read. Join an organization that fights drugs and crime—or that sponsors food drives or visits to nursing homes. This is your town. **Don't sit by when people need help.**

6. The neighbors like trucks; your family likes cars. They dress one way; you all dress another. Maybe they're of a different race and a different religion, too. Many of the most terrible events in human history began with people who looked over the fence at their neighbors and thought, *They're different from me. They shouldn't be like that.* That's bunk. Living with different people makes life more interesting. **Keep your eyes clear and your mind open.**

malls

You've got some money. You've got a ride. You've got some friends. For the next two hours, you and your pals are on your own at the mall. What now?

Elevators

Let people get off before you try to get on. If older people or parents with babies are waiting, hold the door and let them on first.

When getting off an elevator, the people closest to the door go first. If you're near the "door open" button in a crowded elevator, it's nice to push it while people get on and off.

Escalators

A girl who's just remembered that she left her wallet in a changing room at the other end of the mall may brush past other people—if she says, "Excuse me, please." The rest of us should stand quietly and wait.

Doors

Hold doors open for older people, people carrying packages, parents with babies, and other people who look as if they could use a hand.

Saying "thanks" is a way to return the kindness when someone holds a door for you.

Letting a door fall back on the person coming in behind you is inconsiderate. So is goofing around with revolving doors or doors that open automatically.

Some doors love to slam shut with a bang. Try not to let them do it.

Shop nice

People work hard at making displays look good. Don't trash the shelves or put things back on the wrong racks. You're a guest in this store, so act like one.

It's common sense—you don't want to sit near a person who's going to ruin the movie for you. Be sure you don't ruin the movie for someone else, either. We asked some girls how they wanted the person in the next seat to behave, and here's what they said:

Lines

It's OK to save a place in line for a person who is parking the car or meeting you at the theater, or for someone who was standing with you but had to leave for a moment.

It's not OK if you and a pal go to the movies, see a kid you know, and say, "Hey, can we stand with you?"

what do you do?

When you're dealing with strangers, caution comes before anything else.

You're on the Internet, chatting with someone named Meg. "I think we could be friends," she writes. "Tell me about yourself. What's your name? Where do you go to school? Maybe we could get together!"

When you're online, there's simply no way to know for sure whom you're talking to. It's possible for someone to pretend to be a girl when he's not. It's also possible for someone to pretend she's nice when she's not. So no matter how friendly you feel toward Meg, don't give out your last name, your address or phone number, or the name of your school. If she persists, leave the website and talk to your parents about what happened. An incident like this may need to be reported to the people who run the site, and your mom or dad can help you figure out how to do that.

You're at the bus stop with your friends on a busy Saturday. A teenager walks up. He studies the bus map, turns to you, and asks, "Does this bus go to Second Avenue?"

It's a reasonable question. If you know, tell him. If you don't, say, "Sorry, I don't know." It's always good to be careful, but you have friends with you, you're in a public area visible to passersby, and so far this guy is more interested in the map than he is in you. Until he does something more worrisome, you can accept a simple question as just that.

You're buying another notebook. The man at the register says, "Back again, I see. You must really love to write. What's your name? Do you live nearby?"

A little chitchat is natural with strangers to whom you have a reason to talk—a store clerk, a librarian, a bus driver. These conversations should be brief and stick to whatever it is you're doing. They should never be personal. So tell this clerk, "Yes, I like to write," but say nothing about your name or where you live or go to school. If he asks again, it's a bad sign. Leave the store, tell your parents what happened, and start shopping someplace else.

A boy is standing alone on the sidewalk. He goes to your school, but he's two grades ahead. As you pass, he grabs you on the bottom.

Never worry about being polite if someone touches you in any way that feels uncomfortable. Yell **"STOP IT!"** and yell it **LOUD.** Hit him if you need to in order to get away. If he doesn't back off—if he follows you or threatens you—get help from a nearby adult or run to a familiar house or a business. Tell your parents about the incident, and make sure the school knows, too.

good sports

Competition doesn't require leaving your manners on the sidelines.

Winners:

- let their playing do the talking for them.
- don't get mad when things go against them.
- accept the ref's decisions without comment.
- don't show off when they score.
- shake hands with their opponents after the game.
- congratulate one another on their good play.

Losers:

- taunt and swear at other players.
- trade accusations and excuses when they fall behind.
- argue calls with the referee.
- prance and brag after scoring.
- walk away afterward without a word to their opponents.
- blame one another for everything that goes wrong.

In the stands

Stand up for "The Star-Spangled Banner" and all other national anthems. Face the flag, take off your hat, and put your hand on your heart.

Cheer for your favorite team. Do not taunt the competition or use words that make a sporting event sound like a war. No booing. No jeering. These athletes are playing a game. That doesn't give other people the right to insult them.

the great outdoors

You and the rest of the family climb into the car—and you're off. Maybe you're going to a national park a thousand miles away. Maybe you're headed to Lake Wahannamookie for a picnic. Either way, when it's time to climb out, you're going to be a visitor—a tourist, a guest. How are you going to behave? Consider what you would do in the following situations. Be honest!

1. You're walking along a wooded trail when you spot a patch of flowers. They're so pretty! They're so interesting! A sign at the trailhead forbade picking plants, but surely it's OK if you take just one. You do.

a. Yes, that's me.   **b.** I might do this.   **c.** I'd never do this.

2. You buy a candy bar from the vending machine at the rest stop and eat it on the way back to the car. There's no trash can nearby. *Oh well,* you think, *it's just one wrapper. Look at all the stuff other people have dropped around here.* You drop the wrapper.

a. Yes, that's me.   **b.** I might do this.   **c.** I'd never do this.

3. Woo! So this is the Grand Canyon. It's so big! There's a sign telling people not to throw things over the edge because it's unsafe for those below. Still, you wonder . . . No one's watching, so you pick up a rock and pitch it.

a. Yes, that's me.　　**b.** I might do this.　　**c.** I'd never do this.

4. You and your friend are walking along the lake when you see it: a bird's nest hiding in the reeds. It's the tiniest little thing with such pretty eggs. It would look great on your dresser at home. You pick it up.

a. Yes, that's me.　　**b.** I might do this.　　**c.** I'd never do this.

5. The guide says that these Native American ruins have been here for 800 years. Your friend whispers, "Let's carve our initials in this rock to show we were here, too." You do it.

a. Yes, that's me.　　**b.** I might do this.　　**c.** I'd never do this.

6. You're at the beach with your pals—and several thousand other folks. "I brought my radio," you say. "Let's listen to some music." You turn it on and the volume up. Way up.

a. Yes, that's me.　　**b.** I might do this.　　**c.** I'd never do this.

Answers

Natural disaster

If you had more than one **a,** you should take a long, hard look at yourself before you leave the house. You put yourself before other people, treasured monuments, and the environment. You leave a place worse off than it was before you came—and that's super uncool.

"Hello, this is your conscience speaking"

If you had mostly **b's,** you know what's right but are too easily tempted to act selfishly. You can do better!

Invisible girl

If you had mostly **c's,** you're aces in open spaces. You know that when it comes to nature, a girl should enjoy it without leaving a trace that she was ever there.

faraway lands

Pretend you're in another country. Which questions would be considered rude?

3. Why is everything so dirty here?

2. Why don't you speak MY language?

4. Why don't you serve MY food?

1. Why do you dress so funny?

5. Why isn't everything the way it is at home?

Answers

All of them are rude. There isn't a place on the planet where people don't take natural pride in their customs, religions, language, and history. If you behave as if the American way is the only way, it's just plain insulting. Want proof? Then reread these questions, and consider how you would feel if a visitor to this country said the same things to you.

sticky
situations

what do you do?

You avoid sticky situations and embarrassing moments when you can. But how about when you can't?

You're so excited! You've been given two tickets to the concert you and Min-ha have dreamed about. You find her in the hallway, talking to Anna. This is big news! Do you tell her now?

No. You and Min-ha get to do something special, and that's great. But if Anna isn't going to be included in the fun, it's rude to talk about it in front of her. This news can wait, and it should.

A bunch of girls you know are at the pool, and you decide to join them. You're spreading out your towel when Miranda leans over and says, "This is Hannah's birthday party."

You can't crash a party. The question is how to leave without showing the pain and embarrassment you feel. It's going to be hard, but try to pretend this is no big deal. Say "Whoops! I didn't know. Have fun, everybody." Then find a private place where you can recover.

Crash! You've dropped your drink. The glass shatters and juice sprays all over Mrs. Angelini's white carpet.

Tell Mrs. Angelini how sorry you are, and do everything you can to help clean up. Say you're sorry again when you leave, and let your parents know about the spill once you get home. They may want to talk to Mrs. Angelini, too, and perhaps hire a carpet cleaner. Accidents happen—that's just the way it is. If you apologize sincerely and do what you can to put things right, most people will forgive you.

The phone rings. It's Alison. "Want to spend the night?" she asks. You don't want to hurt Alison's feelings, but in your heart of hearts you don't like her very much.

A friendly invitation deserves a friendly reply—even if the reply is no. So use the same tone of voice you would use for a girl you like a lot. Don't say anything hurtful, such as "I don't want to be friends" or "Why are you calling me?" Thank Alison for the invitation when you make your excuse: "I'm sorry, Alison. I have plans. It was nice of you to ask me."

You're at the mall with Tara. She just spent all her money on a headband at the drugstore. Three shops later, you decide to buy a bag of candy. Do you have to share?

It's impolite to eat in front of a person who doesn't have anything to eat herself. You don't have to give Tara half your candy, but you should offer her a few pieces.

You're on your bike when the thought suddenly hits you. Chloe's party! It was today! You said you'd go, and you totally forgot!

Go home, call Chloe, and apologize: "Chloe, I'm so sorry! I forgot about your party. I was looking forward to it, too. I hope my not being there didn't wreck anything. Please forgive me!" Let Chloe be mad at you without getting mad back. Deliver her gift as soon as possible, and include a note apologizing again.

You're having lunch at Debbie's. She is so funny! You laugh and laugh and—OH NOOO! You just wet your pants!

Honesty and humor are the only defense against embarrassment as crushing as this. So say what you're thinking: "This is the most embarrassing thing that's ever happened to me in my whole life." If you can make a joke, that's even better ("I'm going to change my name and move to New Zealand."). Apologize for the mess, clean it up yourself, and accept a change of clothes if it's offered. At that point, Debbie and her family will probably let the subject drop, and so can you.

You'd like to do your homework with Shreya. Can you walk to her house, or do you have to call first?

Call first. Shreya might love to see you, but she might also be doing something with another friend. By calling, you make it easier for Shreya to say no if she wants to. You also avoid creating a situation that could be awkward for you both.

Jordan borrowed your favorite book five weeks ago. You really want it back.

Ask her, in a friendly way, "Are you finished with the book?" If she says yes, ask how she liked it—and add, "Would you please bring the book to school tomorrow? I'd like to have it back." If she says no, give her a deadline: "I'd like to have it back by Tuesday, OK?" Then call Monday night to remind her.

Jacob sits beside you on the bus. He offers you a piece of gum and then says, "Do you want to be my girlfriend?"

"Sure" is one answer. If your parents are OK with your having a boyfriend and you want to be Jacob's girlfriend, you can use that. If you don't want to be Jacob's girlfriend, say no nicely.

special occasions

family gatherings

Extended families get together for holidays and big occasions—births, weddings, funerals, bar and bat mitzvahs, christenings, first communions, and graduations. A family event may mean putting aside your own friends and activities for the day, but it's worth it. You really don't want to miss the moments and memories that bind your family together. So here are some tips for making the most of a family bash.

The star of the day gets the spotlight when it comes to a graduation, birthday, and so on. If you try to compete, jealousy will eat through your day like a worm through an apple.

Your **love means more** to older people than anything in the world. So don't be a miser. When Grandma comes in, throw your arms around her neck and give her a kiss.

Habits differ from family to family. You may be used to eating at 5:30. Your relatives may want to eat at 7:00. You may play horseshoes one way, and your cousin Madi may play it another. If everybody insists on her own way, the visit will be a disaster. Be flexible and compromise.

Be there. Don't spend the visit plugged into a game or your phone.

Bored? Well, sitting around feeling sorry for yourself isn't going to help. Do something. Grab a football and some cousins, and get something going. The one sure way to have a good time is to create one yourself.

Be patient. Big groups can't do anything fast. If you're trying to get 15 people out of the house and into the yard, it's going to take a while. Plan on it.

When the camera comes out, smile. Making faces produces irritated relatives and lousy pictures.

what do you do?

Family get-togethers bring their own kinds of challenges.

Every time my aunt comes to town, my family gets together.
It's all fine until the little kids come. They hound me!
I know they love me, and I love them, but I'm expected
to watch them.
A Girl with No Social Life

Families come with certain obligations, and keeping company with
cousins is one of them. Still, there's no law that says you have to stay
locked in the house, especially if the little kids are around for more than
a day. Talk to your mom about making plans that will include friends
and cousins both. Maybe you and a friend can lead the pack to the
pool, the park, or a movie theater. Or maybe you can cook up a show or
a moneymaking scheme that will entertain everybody—including you.

I am almost twelve years old. At twelve, I will have a celebration called a bat mitzvah. My parents are divorced, and my dad is paying for the celebration. Some of my relatives on my mom's side don't want to come. I'm closer to my mom's side than to my dad's, and I really want them to come. My aunt said we could have a special dinner together instead, but it's not the same.
Upset

Write these relatives a note telling them how you feel. A bat mitzvah is about you—about your growing up and your commitment to your religion. It has nothing to do with your parents' divorce. If these relatives stay away, the only person they're going to hurt is you. Tell them that. Tell them you love them. Then say, "This is important to me. I really want you to come."

weddings

Weddings are as different as the people in them. They can be religious or nonreligious, indoors or outdoors, formal or informal. A traditional wedding consists of a ceremony and a reception. A girl can have a role in the wedding as a bridesmaid or a flower girl. She can also attend as a guest. Either way, she will want her best manners to shine.

Guests

Wedding invitations are usually printed up specially for the event. If a girl is invited, her name will be written on the envelope.

A written reply is required for wedding invitations. So is a gift. Your parents will probably take care of both.

Generally, the later in the day a wedding takes place, the fancier it is. A wedding designated "black tie" or "white tie" is very fancy indeed. Keep this in mind when you're deciding what to wear.

Bridesmaids

Being a bridesmaid gets you a special dress—and special responsibilities.

There is always at least one rehearsal for the members of the wedding party. That's when you find out what you'll need to do. Listen up and ask questions then, because there won't be time to do so in the hectic moments before the start of the wedding.

Getting seated

Guests are seated by an usher—usually family and friends of the groom on one side of the aisle, family and friends of the bride on the other. In traditional Christian services, the mothers of the bride and groom are seated individually just before the ceremony starts. (That's how guests know it's about to begin.)

The bridal party

The bridal party, or wedding party, is made up of everybody who stands at the front with the bride and groom during the ceremony. This includes the ushers and best man, who are usually brothers or good friends of the groom, and the bridesmaids, who are usually sisters or good friends of the bride. It may also include a ring bearer (a young boy who's entrusted with carrying the wedding rings) and a flower girl (a girl age eight or younger who walks ahead of the bride).

The procession

The exact order in which members of the wedding party move to the front depends on both religion and preference. Usually bridesmaids and flower girls go down the aisle before the bride. The trick is not to rush it.

A girl should walk slowly—gracefully, calmly—with a smile on her face. Last of all (ta-da!) comes the bride, often on her father's arm. When she appears, the guests stand.

The vows

The couple make promises about the life they will lead, reflecting the love they feel for each other. Often they exchange rings. In a Jewish wedding, the pair stand under a canopy called a *chuppah* (HUHP-pa), and the groom breaks a glass wrapped in a napkin as a reminder of the sorrows the Jewish people have experienced.

What should guests and members of the wedding party do during the ceremony? Listen quietly, of course.

The receiving line

Members of the wedding party often stand in a line after the ceremony while guests file past one by one. Guests should move down the line quickly, shaking hands, congratulating the bride and groom, greeting people they know, and introducing themselves to people they don't know.

A bridesmaid in the receiving line can expect to meet and greet lots and lots of people. Her job is to stay cheerful and friendly the entire time. Once all the guests have gone through the line, the members of the wedding party are free to join the reception.

The reception

A reception is a party. It can be anything from a simple get-together in a church hall to a big sit-down dinner someplace fancy. Sometimes, toasts are made to the bride and groom. (The adults may drink wine or champagne with each toast. A girl can drink juice or water.) At some point, the newlyweds cut the wedding cake.

Often there's music and dancing. The bride and groom dance the first dance alone. After that, everyone else can join in—including you.

Farewell

When the bride and groom are getting ready to leave, the bride tosses her bouquet into a group of unmarried women and girls. If you're included, jump like a WNBA All-Star but don't push and shove like a tackle in the NFL.

As the couple make their way out, well-wishers may shower them—gently!—with rice, birdseed, bubbles, or confetti.

funerals

If you've never been to a funeral, the whole idea may make you nervous. Don't be. Funerals are sad and serious occasions, but they need not be frightening. The whole point is to help comfort people who have lost someone dear to them. A funeral affirms the religious beliefs of the family. It celebrates the life of the person who died and the love that lives on.

Behavior

Keep your voice low and behave seriously. Loud talking and laughing are insulting to the feelings of others.

At some funerals, the body of the person who died is on display in the coffin. You don't need to approach the coffin if you don't want to. If you do, pause for a moment to think about the person and what he or she meant to you.

Dress

Dress nicely. You don't need to wear black, but this isn't the time to wear your wildest, brightest outfit, either.

Guest book

At many funerals there is a guest book, in which people attending the ceremony sign their names. The book is a keepsake for the family.

Receiving line

Either before or after the ceremony, there may be a receiving line, where members of the family greet other people. When you go through a receiving line, shake hands and introduce yourself. Say something about what the dead person meant to you: "Mr. Hornbeck was the best teacher I ever had. I'll always remember him."

Tears

You may see people crying; you may cry yourself. This is natural. Don't feel ashamed to let your sadness show, and don't feel alarmed if others express their grief, either. It's a good idea to bring some tissues with you.

Home visits

There may be an informal gathering at the family's home after the funeral. Visits to the home may occur at other times as well. If the family is Christian, there may be a gathering the night before the funeral. This is called a *wake*. If the family is Jewish, the family may stay at home for a number of days after the funeral, a tradition called sitting *shiva*. This is also a period when friends and relatives may visit.

A home visit calls for the same kind of manners you bring to the funeral itself—quiet and respectful.

What can you say to a friend who's lost someone she loved? And what can you do that might make things easier for her? Girls who have had to deal with death have these things to say about how friends can help:

"Even if all you say is 'I'm sorry,' you should say it. You'd be surprised at how nice it feels to know that someone cares."
Emily

"When my loved one died, I got lots of 'sorry's from kids at school. It was nice of them to think of me, but one of my friends wrote me a letter. It really made me feel that if I needed anyone to talk to, she was there for me."
Marisa

"My grandfather died of cancer. When I went back to school, one of my friends said, 'I guess you don't want to talk about it.' But that wasn't true. I did want to talk. Often, remembering things about the person can make you feel a little less sad."
Julia

"My father died two years ago this summer. When I went to school that year, everybody said they were sorry. One person told me she would always remember my dad. That really touched me."
Heather

"When my dad died, my classmates sent me an ornament of flowers. I still have it today, and that was seven years ago."
Madison

"If you know someone who has lost a loved one, bring her family food. Usually the family is too sad to cook."
Jessica

protocol

When it comes to high officials, a lot of special rules apply. These rules are called *protocol*. Protocol encourages respect for positions of authority—for presidents and kings, senators and judges, generals and diplomats. In places like Washington, DC, where such people tend to turn up, protocol determines things such as who goes first and proper forms of address. It's nothing to be scared of. If you're invited to a fancy government event, simply ask your parents about what's expected.

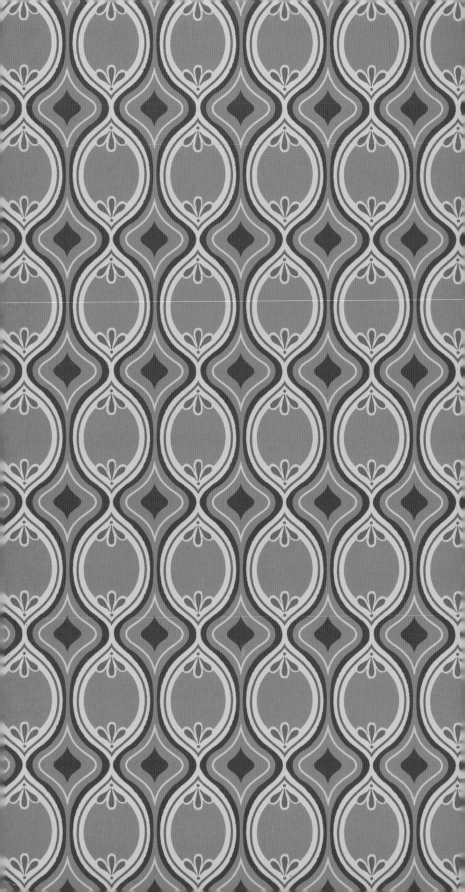